The Organist's Picture Chords

Here in this book are illustrated (both with keyboard diagrams and actual photographs) the most commonly used chords in music, as they would be played on organ.

The chords are set out for the **Left Hand** on the **Lower Keyboard.** (The Right Hand of course will be playing the **Melody** on the Upper Keyboard, or higher up the keyboard on a single-keyboard organ).

Two Pedal Notes are given for each chord (only applicable of course to organs with pedals). The first Pedal Note given is the most important, being the Fundamental Bass Note, or "Root" of the chord. The second Pedal Note (the "Alternate" pedal) provides a nice alternative, especially useful when playing rhythmically (as in Waltzes, Foxtrots, etc.).

The fingerings given are the usual ones but certain chord progressions could call for slightly different fingerings here and there.

Hal Leonard

Exclusive distributors:
Hal Leonard,
7777 West Bluemound Road,
Milwaukee, WI 53213
Email: info@halleonard.com
Hal Leonard Europe Limited,
42 Wigmore Street Marylebone,
London, WIU 2 RY
Email: info@halleonardeurope.com
Hal Leonard Australia Pty. Ltd.
4 Lentara Court Cheltenham,
Victoria 9132, Australia
Email: info@halleonard.com.au

Designed by Howard Brown.
Photographs by Roger Perry.

A

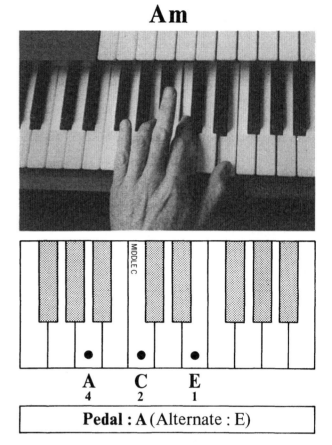

A **C#** **E**
4   2   1

Pedal : A (Alternate : E)

Am

A **C** **E**
4   2   1

Pedal : A (Alternate : E)

Aaug (A+)

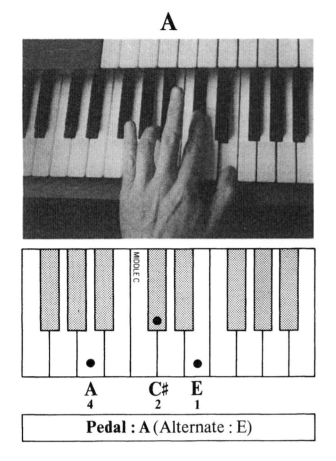

E#(F) **A** **C#**
5   3   1

Pedal : A (Alternate : E#(F))

Adim (A°)

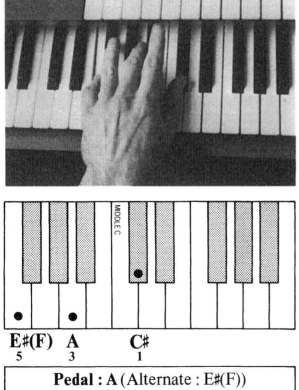

Gb **C** **Eb**
5   2   1

Pedal : A (Alternate : Eb)

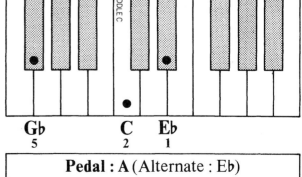

A

A7

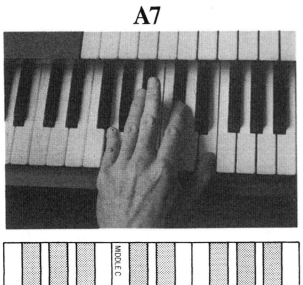

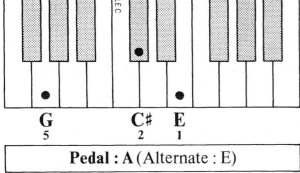

G **C#** **E**
5 2 1

Pedal : A (Alternate : E)

Am7

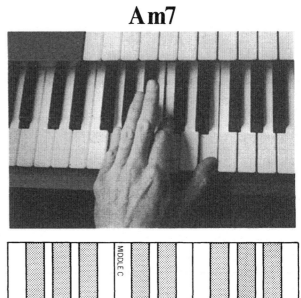

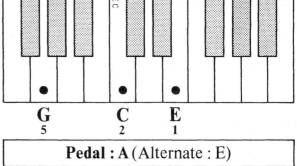

G **C** **E**
5 2 1

Pedal : A (Alternate : E)

A6

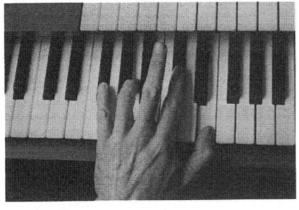

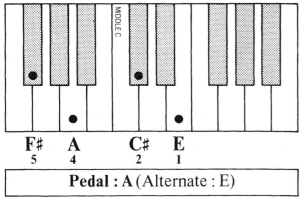

F# **A** **C#** **E**
5 4 2 1

Pedal : A (Alternate : E)

Am6

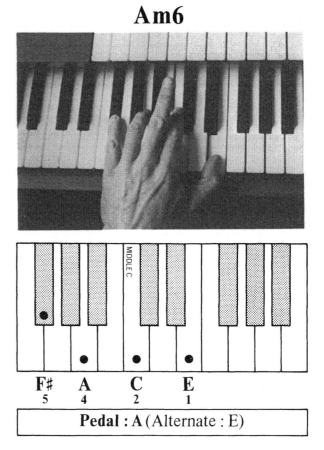

F# **A** **C** **E**
5 4 2 1

Pedal : A (Alternate : E)

Bb

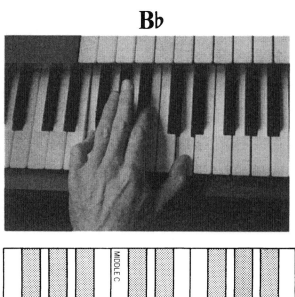

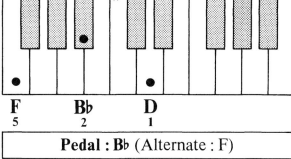

F 5   Bb 2   D 1

Pedal : Bb (Alternate : F)

Bbm

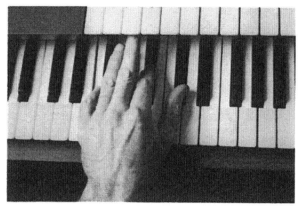

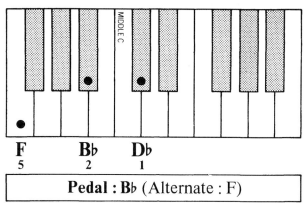

F 5   Bb 2   Db 1

Pedal : Bb (Alternate : F)

Bbaug (Bb+)

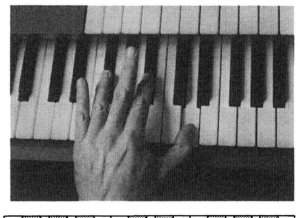

F# 4   Bb 2   D 1

Pedal : Bb (Alternate : F#)

Bbdim (Bb°) (A#dim) (A#°)

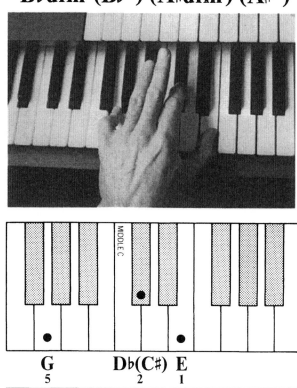

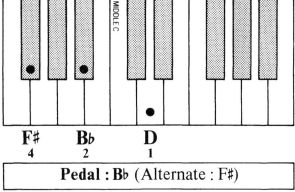

G 5   Db(C#) 2   E 1

Pedal : Bb (Alternate : E)

Bb

Bb7

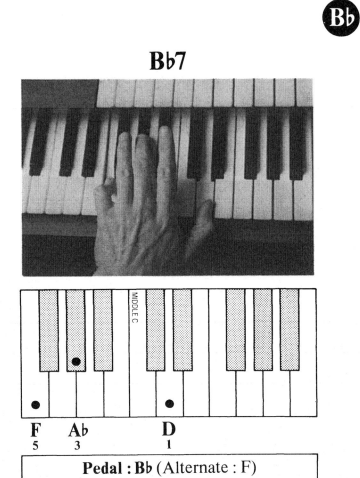

F	Ab	D
5	3	1

Pedal : Bb (Alternate : F)

Bbm7

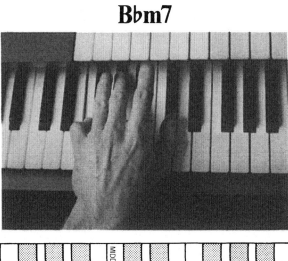

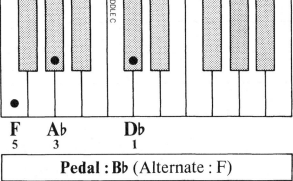

F	Ab	Db
5	3	1

Pedal : Bb (Alternate : F)

Bb6

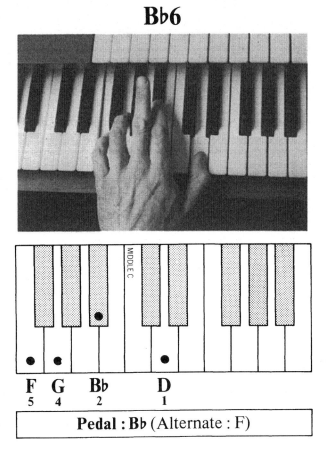

F	G	Bb	D
5	4	2	1

Pedal : Bb (Alternate : F)

Bbm6

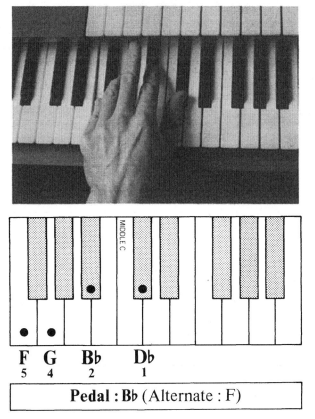

F	G	Bb	Db
5	4	2	1

Pedal : Bb (Alternate : F)

B

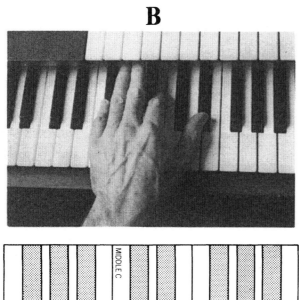

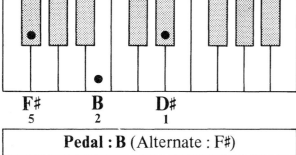

F# · B · D#
5 · 2 · 1

Pedal : B (Alternate : F#)

Bm

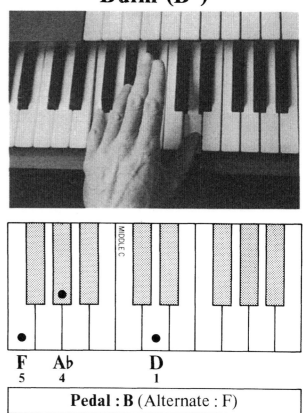

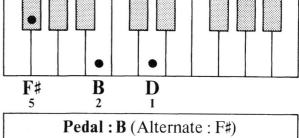

F# · B · D
5 · 2 · 1

Pedal : B (Alternate : F#)

Baug (B+)

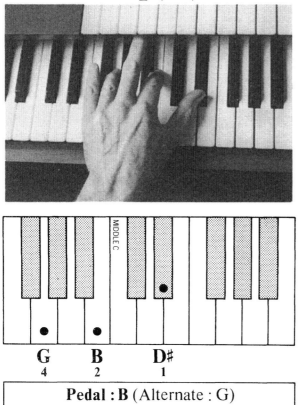

G · B · D#
4 · 2 · 1

Pedal : B (Alternate : G)

Bdim (B°)

F · Ab · D
5 · 4 · 1

Pedal : B (Alternate : F)

B7

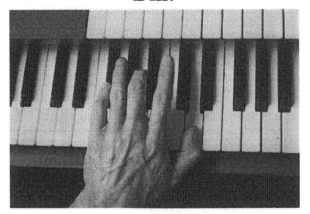

F# A   D#
5   3   1
Pedal : B (Alternate : F#)

Bm7

F# A   D
5   3   1
Pedal : B (Alternate : F#)

B6

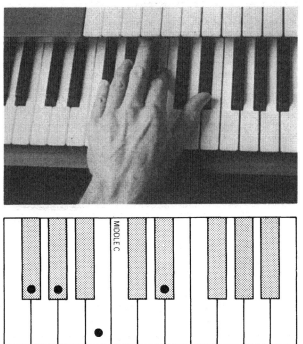

F# G# B   D#
5 4   2   1
Pedal : B (Alternate : F#)

Bm6

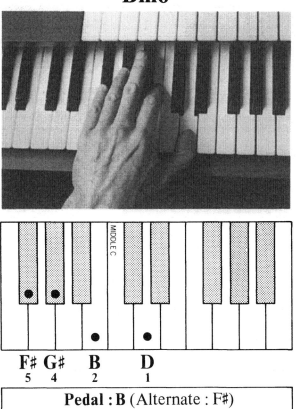

F# G# B   D
5 4   2   1
Pedal : B (Alternate : F#)

C

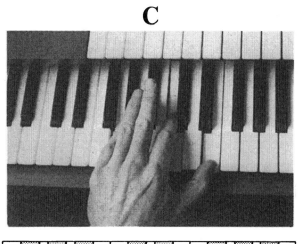

G 5 C 2 E 1

Pedal : C (Alternate : G)

Cm

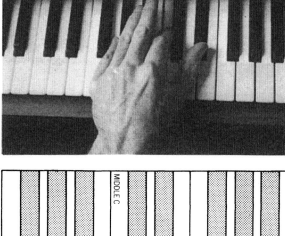

G 5 C 2 E♭ 1

Pedal : C (Alternate : G)

Caug (C+)

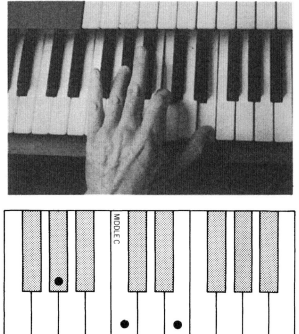

G♯ 4 C 2 E 1

Pedal : C (Alternate : G♯)

Cdim (C°)

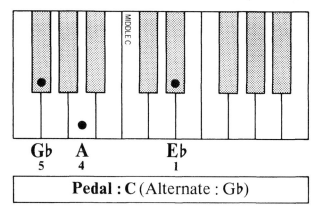

G♭ 5 A 4 E♭ 1

Pedal : C (Alternate : G♭)

C

C7

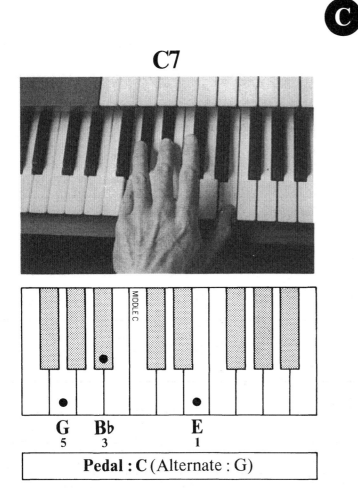

G	B♭	E
5	3	1

Pedal : C (Alternate : G)

Cm7

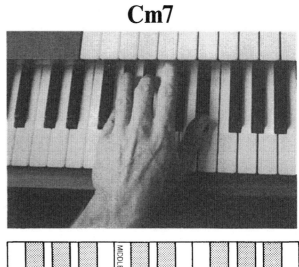

G	B♭	E♭
5	3	1

Pedal : C (Alternate : G)

C6

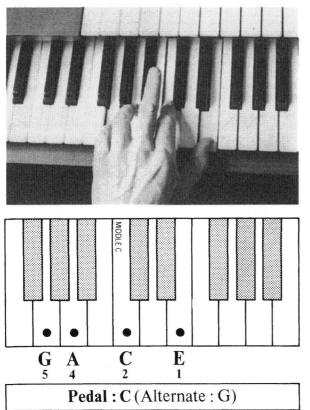

G	A	C	E
5	4	2	1

Pedal : C (Alternate : G)

Cm6

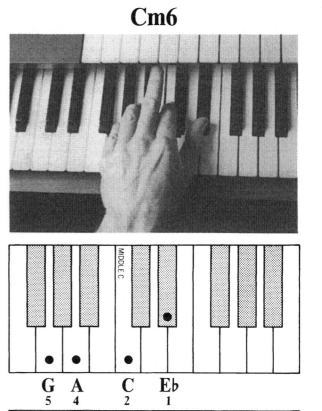
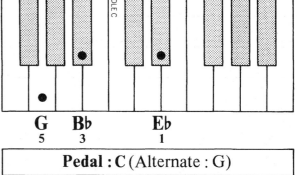

G	A	C	E♭
5	4	2	1

Pedal : C (Alternate : G)

C#

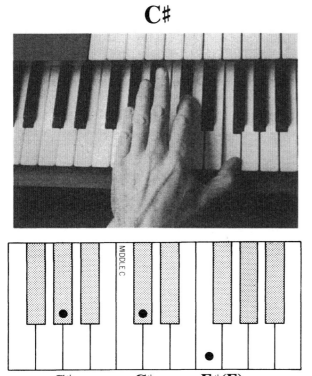

G#
5

C#
2

E#(F)
1

Pedal : C#(Alternate : G#)

C#m

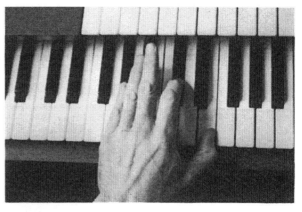

G#
5

C#
2

E
1

Pedal : C#(Alternate : G#)

C#aug (C#+)

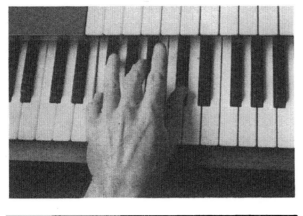

E#(F)
5

G×(A)
3

C#
1

Pedal : C#(Alternate : G×(A))

C#dim (C#°)

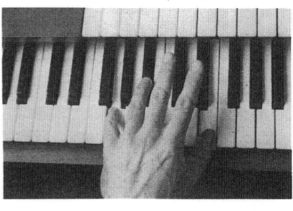

G
5

B♭
4

E
1

Pedal : C#(Alternate : G)

C#7

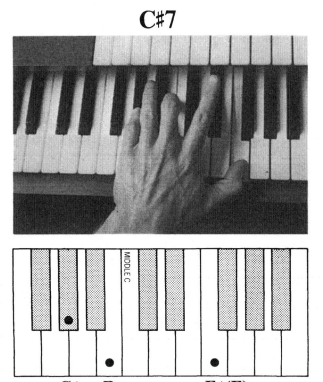

G#   B   E#(F)
5   3   1

Pedal : C# (Alternate : G#)

C#m7

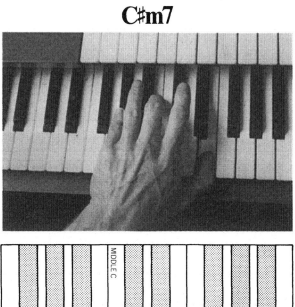

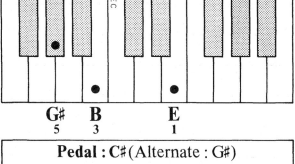

G#   B   E
5   3   1

Pedal : C# (Alternate : G#)

C#6

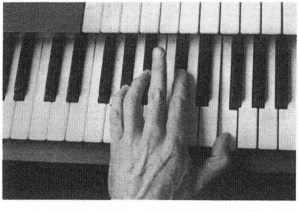

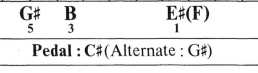

G#   A#   C#   E#(F)
5   4   2   1

Pedal : C# (Alternate : G#)

C#m6

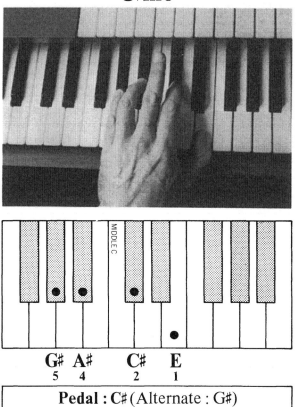

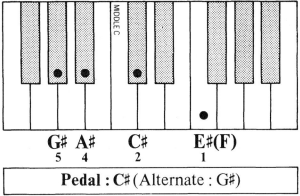

G#   A#   C#   E
5   4   2   1

Pedal : C# (Alternate : G#)

Db

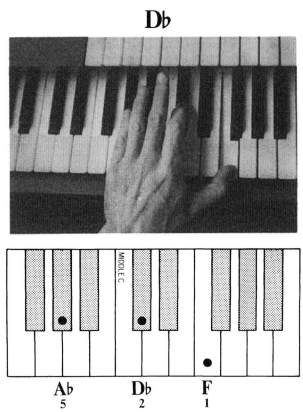

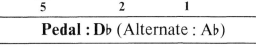

Ab **Db** **F**
5   2   1

Pedal : Db (Alternate : Ab)

Dbm

Ab **Db** **Fb(E)**
5   2   1

Pedal : Db (Alternate : Ab)

Dbaug (Db+)

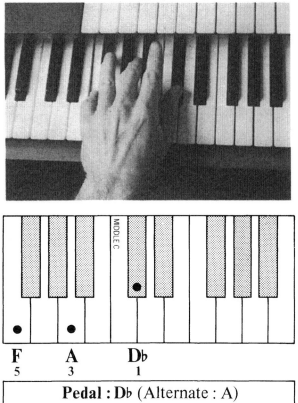

F **A** **Db**
5   3   1

Pedal : Db (Alternate : A)

Dbdim (Db°)

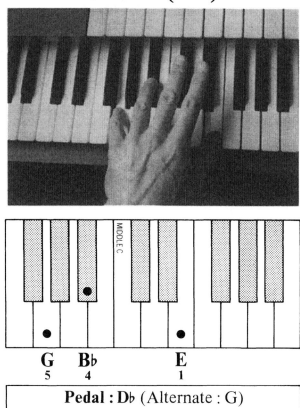

G **Bb** **E**
5   4   1

Pedal : Db (Alternate : G)

Db

Db7

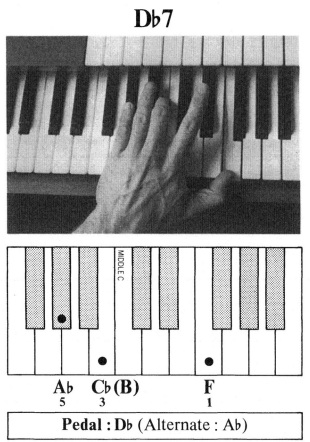

Ab	Cb(B)	F
5	3	1

Pedal : Db (Alternate : Ab)

Dbm7

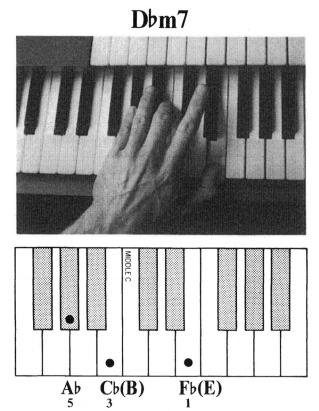

Ab	Cb(B)	Fb(E)
5	3	1

Pedal : Db (Alternate : Ab)

Db6

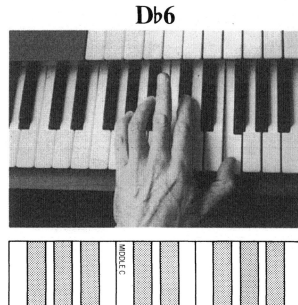

Ab	Bb	Db	F
5	4	2	1

Pedal : Db (Alternate : Ab)

Dbm6

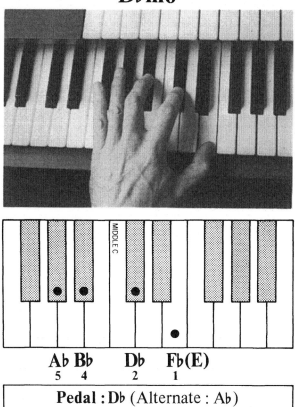

Ab	Bb	Db	Fb(E)
5	4	2	1

Pedal : Db (Alternate : Ab)

D

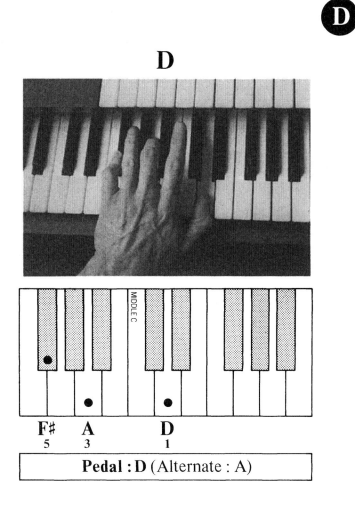

F♯
5

A
3

D
1

Pedal : D (Alternate : A)

Dm

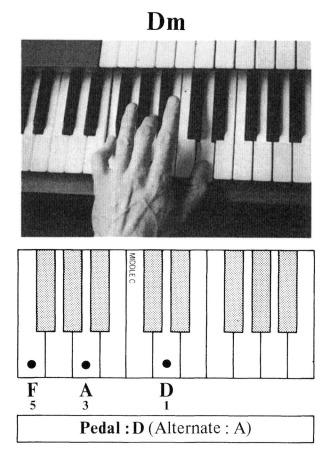

F
5

A
3

D
1

Pedal : D (Alternate : A)

Daug (D+)

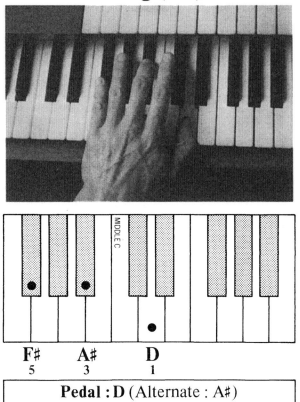

F♯
5

A♯
3

D
1

Pedal : D (Alternate : A♯)

Ddim (D°)

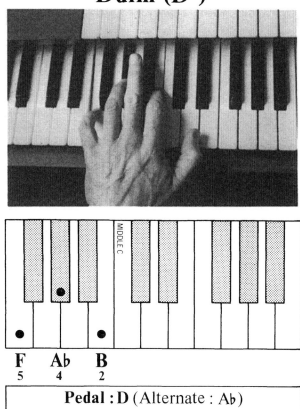

F
5

A♭
4

B
2

Pedal : D (Alternate : A♭)

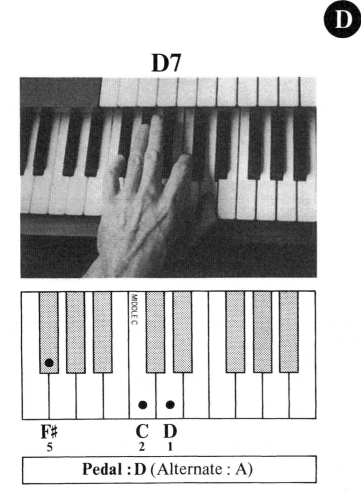

D7

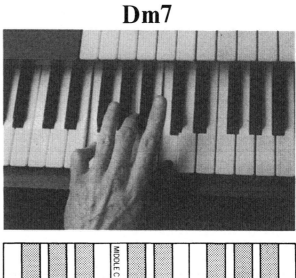

F♯			C	D
5			2	1

Pedal : D (Alternate : A)

Dm7

F		A		C
5		3		1

Pedal : D (Alternate : A)

D6

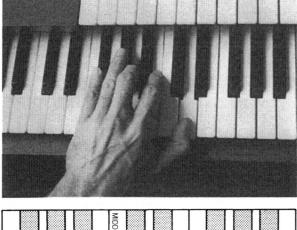

F♯		A	B		D
5		3	2		1

Pedal : D (Alternate : A)

Dm6

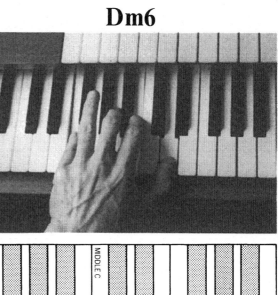

F		A	B		D
5		3	2		1

Pedal : D (Alternate : A)

E♭

G	B♭	E♭
5	3	1

Pedal : E♭ (Alternate : B♭)

E♭m

G♭	B♭	E♭
5	3	1

Pedal : E♭ (Alternate : B♭)

E♭aug (E♭+)

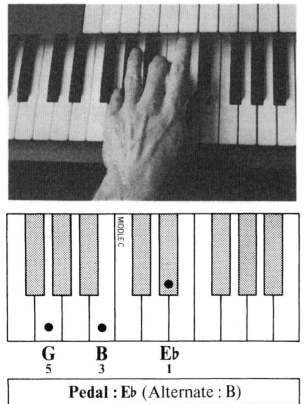

G	B	E♭
5	3	1

Pedal : E♭ (Alternate : B)

E♭dim (E♭°) (D♯dim) (D♯°)

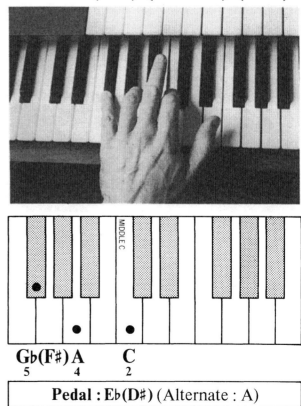

G♭(F♯)	A	C
5	4	2

Pedal : E♭(D♯) (Alternate : A)

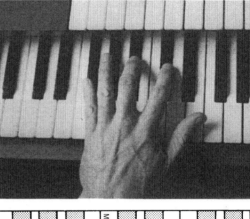

Eb7

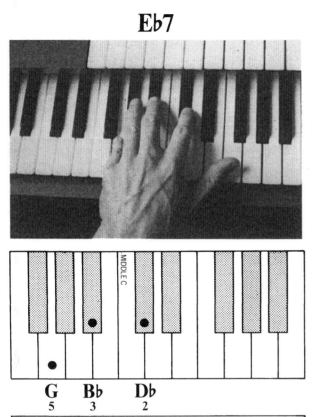

G **Bb** **Db**
5   3   2

Pedal : Eb (Alternate : Bb)

Ebm7

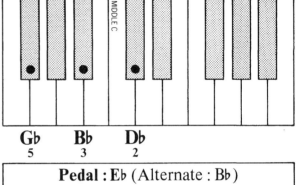

Gb **Bb** **Db**
5   3   2

Pedal : Eb (Alternate : Bb)

Eb6

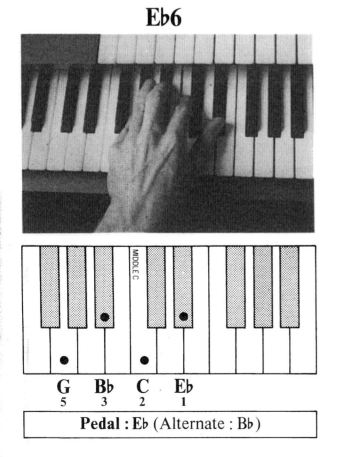

G **Bb** **C** **Eb**
5   3   2   1

Pedal : Eb (Alternate : Bb)

Ebm6

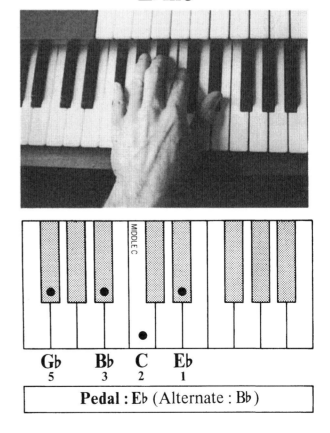

Gb **Bb** **C** **Eb**
5   3   2   1

Pedal : Eb (Alternate : Bb)

E

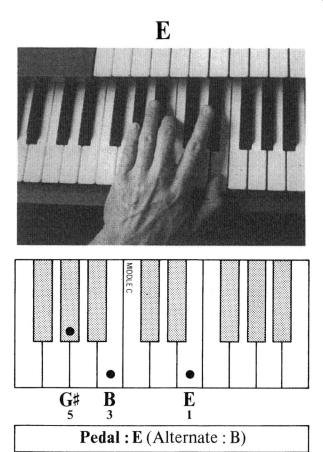

G# **B** **E**
5   3   1

Pedal : E (Alternate : B)

Em

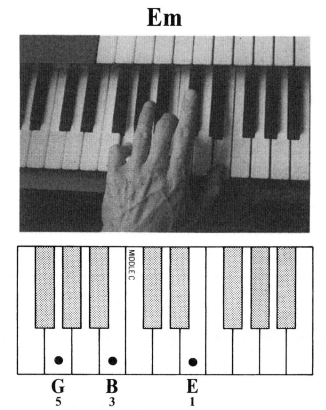

G **B** **E**
5   3   1

Pedal : E (Alternate : B)

Eaug (E+)

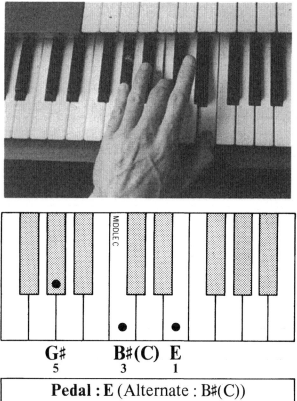

G# **B#(C)** **E**
5   3   1

Pedal : E (Alternate : B#(C))

Edim (E°)

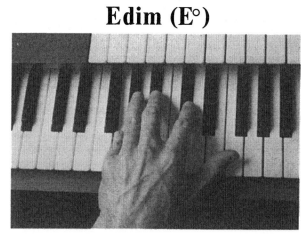
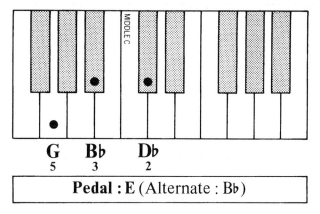

G **Bb** **Db**
5   3   2

Pedal : E (Alternate : Bb)

E7

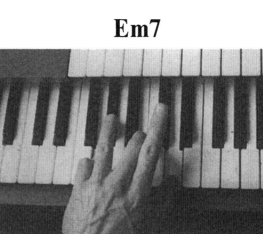

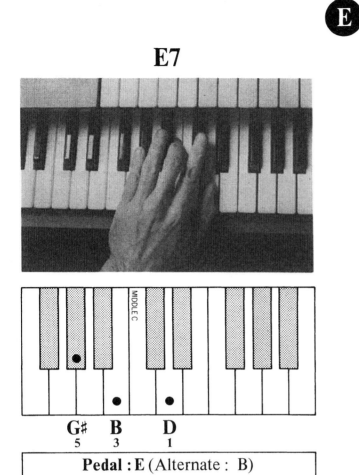

G# **B** **D**
5   3   1

Pedal : E (Alternate : B)

Em7

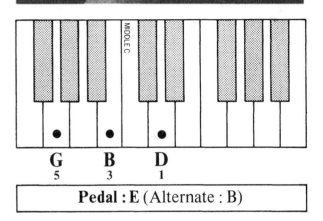

G **B** **D**
5   3   1

Pedal : E (Alternate : B)

E6

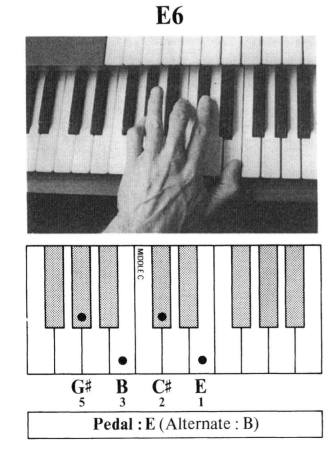

G# **B** **C#** **E**
5   3   2   1

Pedal : E (Alternate : B)

Em6

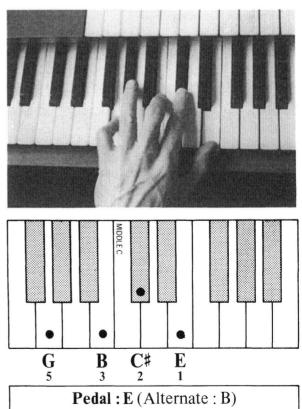

G **B** **C#** **E**
5   3   2   1

Pedal : E (Alternate : B)

F

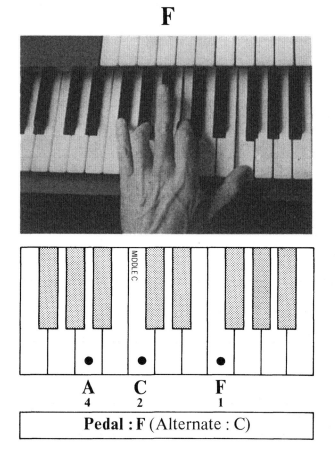

A 4   C 2   F 1

Pedal : F (Alternate : C)

Fm

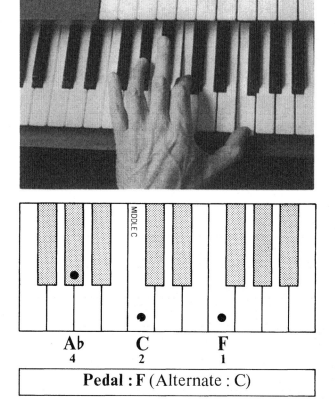

A♭ 4   C 2   F 1

Pedal : F (Alternate : C)

Faug (F+)

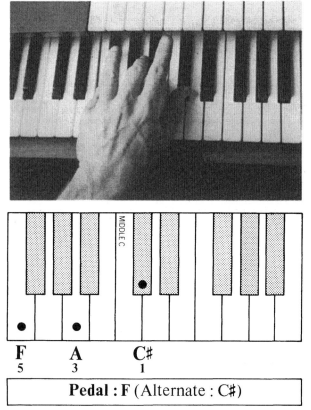

F 5   A 3   C♯ 1

Pedal : F (Alternate : C♯)

Fdim (F°)

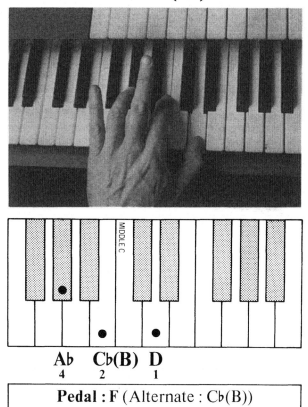

A♭ 4   C♭(B) 2   D 1

Pedal : F (Alternate : C♭(B))

F7

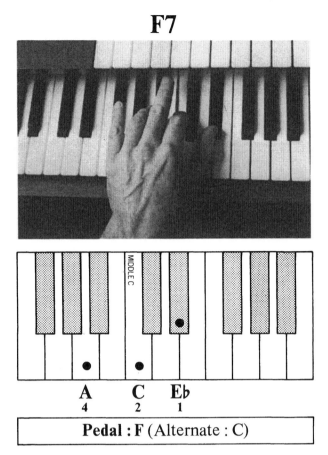

A — 4
C — 2
E♭ — 1

Pedal : F (Alternate : C)

Fm7

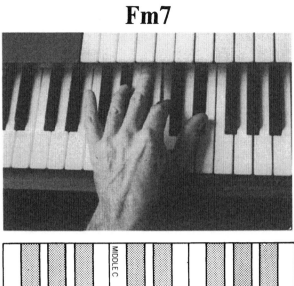
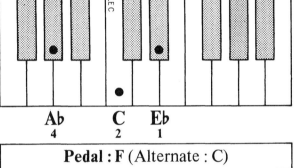

A♭ — 4
C — 2
E♭ — 1

Pedal : F (Alternate : C)

F6

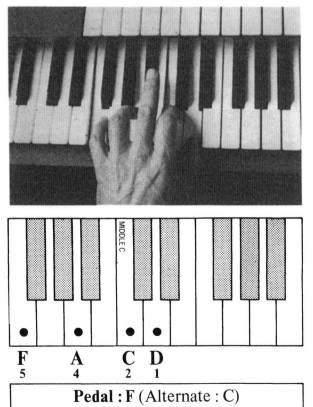

F — 5
A — 4
C — 2
D — 1

Pedal : F (Alternate : C)

Fm6

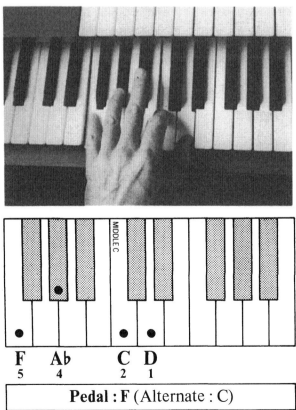

F — 5
A♭ — 4
C — 2
D — 1

Pedal : F (Alternate : C)

F#

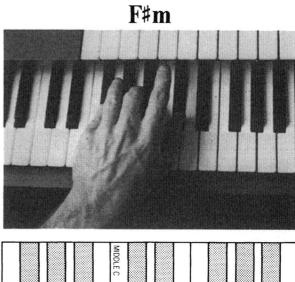

F# A# C#
5   3   1

Pedal : F# (Alternate : C#)

F#m

F# A C#
5   3   1

Pedal : F# (Alternate : C#)

F#aug (F#+)

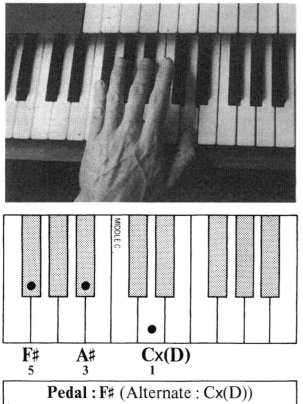

F# A# Cx(D)
5   3   1

Pedal : F# (Alternate : Cx(D))

F#dim (F#°)

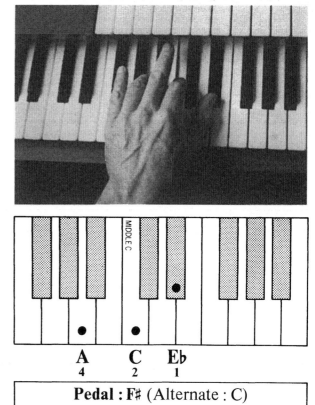

A   C   Eb
4   2   1

Pedal : F# (Alternate : C)

F#7

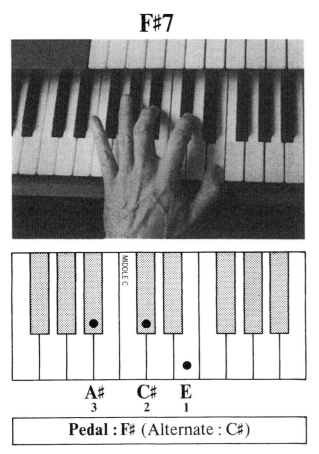

A# **C#** **E**
3 2 1

Pedal : F# (Alternate : C#)

F#m7

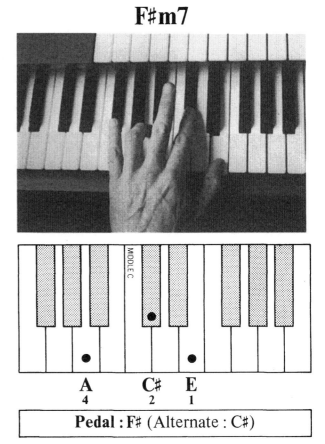

A **C#** **E**
4 2 1

Pedal : F# (Alternate : C#)

F#6

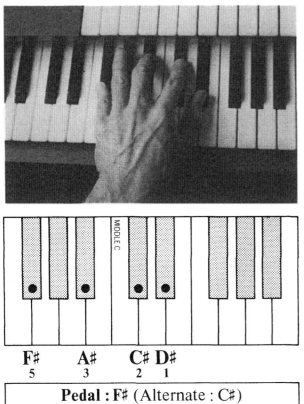

F# **A#** **C# D#**
5 3 2 1

Pedal : F# (Alternate : C#)

F#m6

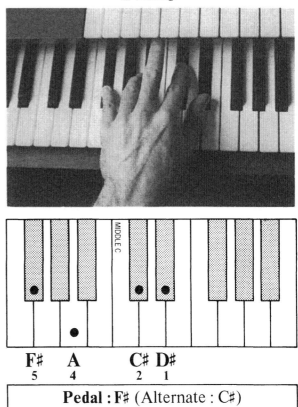

F# **A** **C# D#**
5 4 2 1

Pedal : F# (Alternate : C#)

Gb

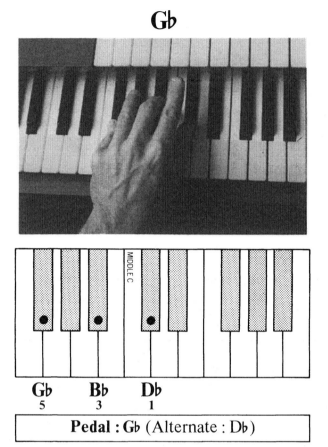

Gb **Bb** **Db**
5   3   1

Pedal : Gb (Alternate : Db)

Gbm

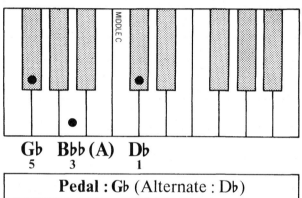

Gb **Bbb (A)** **Db**
5   3   1

Pedal : Gb (Alternate : Db)

Gbaug (Gb+)

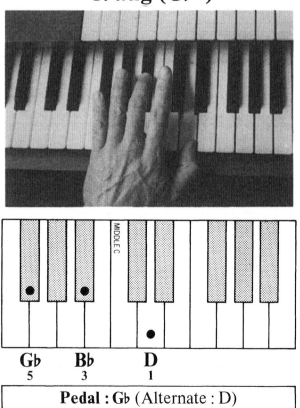

Gb **Bb** **D**
5   3   1

Pedal : Gb (Alternate : D)

Gbdim (Gb°)

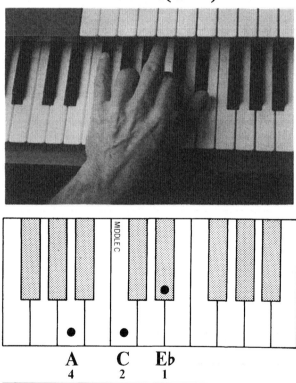

A **C** **Eb**
4   2   1

Pedal : Gb (Alternate : C)

Gb7

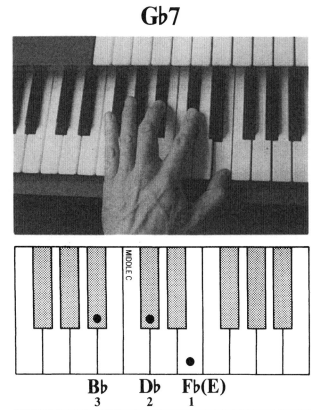

Bb Db Fb(E)
3   2   1

Pedal : Gb (Alternate : Db)

Gbm7

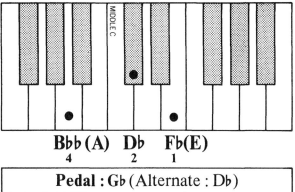

Bbb (A) Db Fb(E)
4   2   1

Pedal : Gb (Alternate : Db)

Gb6

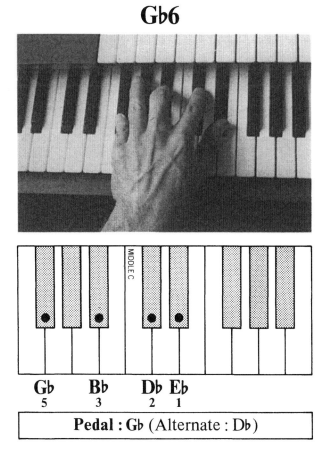

Gb Bb Db Eb
5   3   2 1

Pedal : Gb (Alternate : Db)

Gbm6

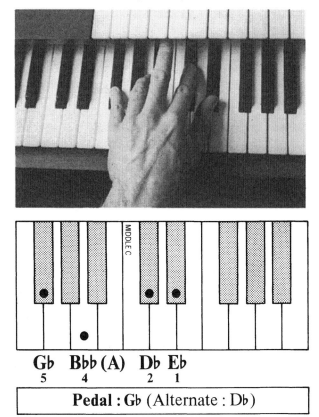

Gb Bbb (A) Db Eb
5   4   2 1

Pedal : Gb (Alternate : Db)

G

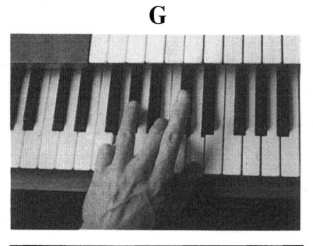

G   B   D
5   3   1

Pedal : G (Alternate : D)

Gm

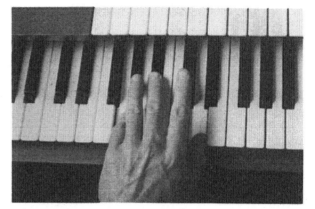

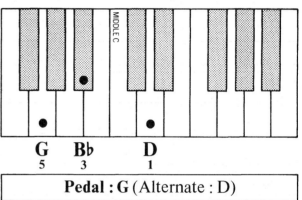

G   B♭   D
5   3   1

Pedal : G (Alternate : D)

Gaug (G+)

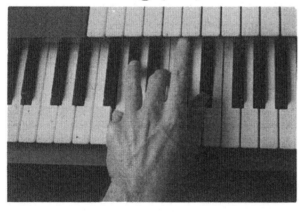

G   B   D♯
5   3   1

Pedal : G (Alternate : D♯)

Gdim (G°)

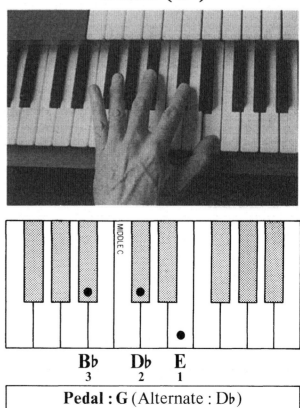

B♭   D♭   E
3   2   1

Pedal : G (Alternate : D♭)

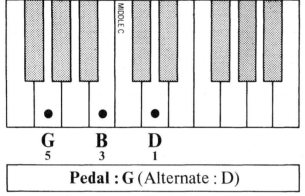
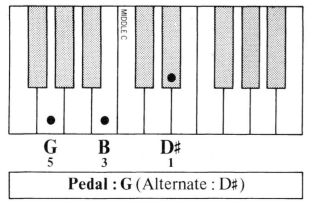

G7

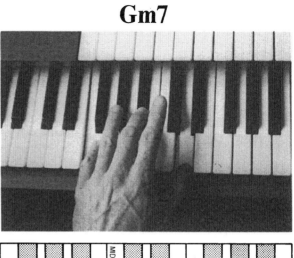

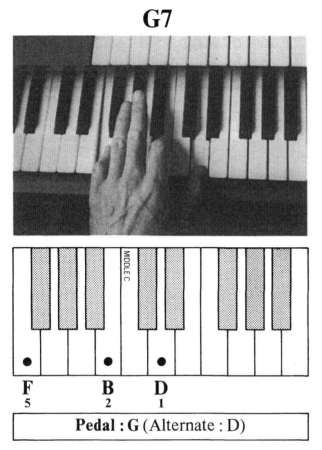

F 5   B 2   D 1

Pedal : G (Alternate : D)

Gm7

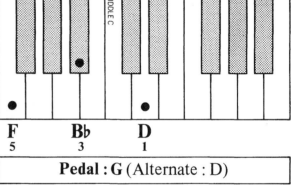

F 5   Bb 3   D 1

Pedal : G (Alternate : D)

G6

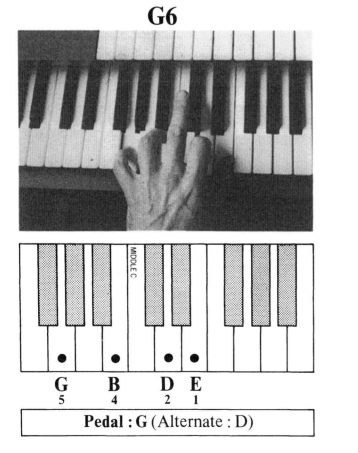

G 5   B 4   D 2   E 1

Pedal : G (Alternate : D)

Gm6

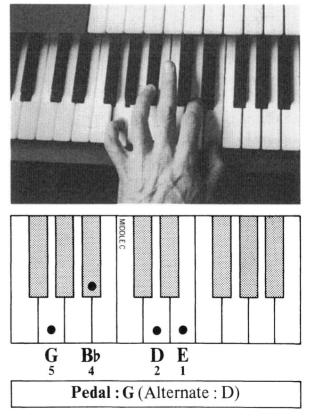

G 5   Bb 4   D 2   E 1

Pedal : G (Alternate : D)

Ab

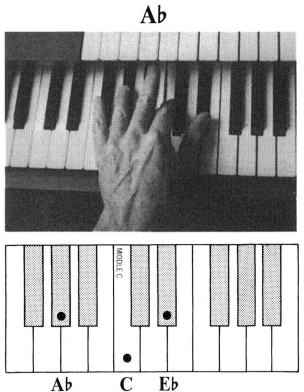

Ab
4

C
2

Eb
1

Pedal : Ab (Alternate : Eb)

Abm

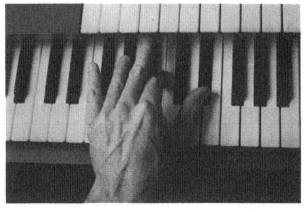

Ab
4

Cb(B)
2

Eb
1

Pedal : Ab (Alternate : Eb)

Abaug (Ab+)

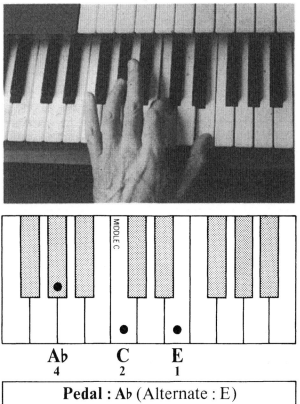

Ab
4

C
2

E
1

Pedal : Ab (Alternate : E)

Abdim (Ab°) (G♯dim) (G♯°)

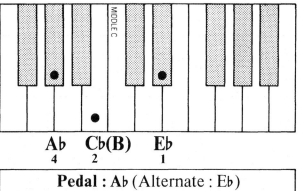

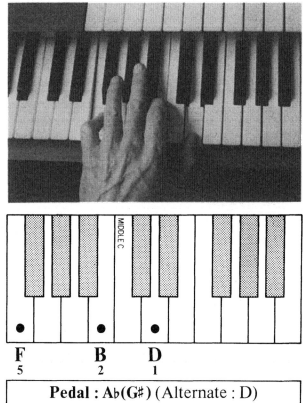

F
5

B
2

D
1

Pedal : Ab(G♯) (Alternate : D)

Ab7

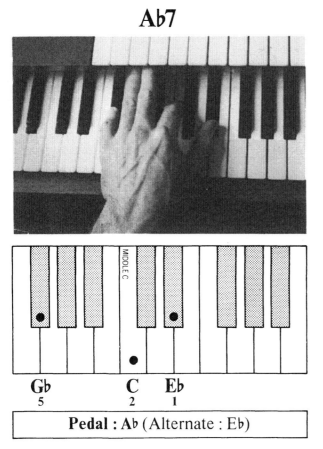

Gb 5 C 2 Eb 1

Pedal : A♭ (Alternate : E♭)

Abm7

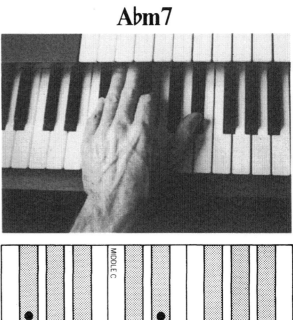

Gb 5 Cb(B) 2 Eb 1

Pedal : A♭ (Alternate : E♭)

Ab6

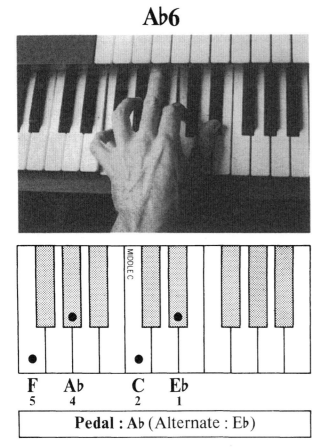

F 5 Ab 4 C 2 Eb 1

Pedal : A♭ (Alternate : E♭)

Abm6

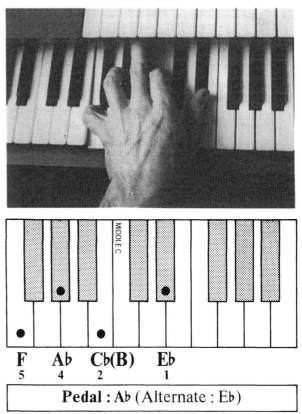

F 5 Ab 4 Cb(B) 2 Eb 1

Pedal : A♭ (Alternate : E♭)

Common Chord Progressions

Key C

1. ‖: C | C7 | F | Fm | C | G7 | C | G7 :‖ *

2. ‖: C | Am | Dm | G7 :‖ or: ‖:C6 | Am7 | Dm7 | G7 :‖

3. ‖: C | C#° | Dm7 | G7 | C(E Pedal) | Eb° | Dm7 | G7 :‖

4. ‖: C | B7 | E7 | A7 | D7 | G7 | C | G7 :‖

5. ‖: Gb7 | F7 | Em7 | Eb7 | Dm7 | Db7 | C | ∕∕ ** :‖

*Repeat whole line **Repeat previous bar

Key F

1. ‖: F | F7 | Bb | Bbm | F | C7 | F | C7 :‖

2. ‖: F | Dm | Gm | C7 :‖ or: ‖:F6 | Dm7 | Gm7 | C7 :‖

3. ‖: F | F#° | Gm7 | C7 | F(A Pedal) | Ab° | Gm7 | C7 :‖

4. ‖: F | E7 | A7 | D7 | G7 | C7 | F | C7 :‖

5. ‖: B7 | Bb7 | Am7 | Ab7 | Gm7 | Gb7 | F | ∕∕ :‖

Key G

1. ‖: G | G7 | C | Cm | G | D7 | G | D7 :‖

2. ‖: G | Em | Am | D7 :‖ or: ‖:G6 | Em7 | Am7 | D7 :‖

3. ‖: G | G#° | Am7 | D7 | G(B Pedal) | Bb° | Am7 | D7 :‖

4. ‖: G | F#7 | B7 | E7 | A7 | D7 | G | D7 :‖

5. ‖: Db7 | C7 | Bm7 | Bb7 | Am7 | Ab7 | G | ∕∕ :‖

Key B♭

1. ‖: B♭ | B♭7 | E♭ | E♭m | B♭ | F7 | B♭ | F7 :‖

2. ‖: B♭ | Gm | Cm | F7 :‖ or: ‖: B♭6 | Gm7 | Cm7 | F7 :‖

3. ‖: B♭ | B° | Cm7 | F7 | B♭(D Pedal) | D♭° | Cm7 | F7 :‖

4. ‖: B♭ | A7 | D7 | G7 | C7 | F7 | B♭ | F7 :‖

5. ‖: E7 | E♭7 | Dm7 | D♭7 | Cm7 | B7 | B♭ | ∕. :‖

Key E♭

1. ‖: E♭ | E♭7 | A♭ | A♭m | E♭ | B♭7 | E♭ | B♭7 :‖

2. ‖: E♭ | Cm | Fm | B♭7 :‖ or: ‖: E♭6 | Cm7 | Fm7 | B♭7 :‖

3. ‖: E♭ | E° | Fm7 | B♭7 | E♭(G Pedal) | G♭° | Fm7 | B♭7 :‖

4. ‖: E♭ | D7 | G7 | C7 | F7 | B♭7 | E♭ | B♭7 :‖

5. ‖: A7 | A♭7 | Gm7 | G♭7 | Fm7 | E7 | E♭ | ∕. :‖

Key Am

‖: Am | Dm | E7 | Am :‖ or: ‖: Am6 | Dm6 | E7 | Am6 :‖

Key Dm

‖: Dm | Gm | A7 | Dm :‖ or: ‖: Dm6 | Gm6 | A7 | Dm6 :‖

Key Em

‖: Em | Am | B7 | Em :‖ or: ‖: Em6 | Am6 | B7 | Em6 :‖

Key Gm

‖: Gm | Cm | D7 | Gm :‖ or: ‖: Gm6 | Cm6 | D7 | Gm6 :‖

Key Cm

‖: Cm | Fm | G7 | Cm :‖ or: ‖: Cm6 | Fm6 | G7 | Cm6 :‖

Twelve-bar Blues

Key C

‖: $\frac{4}{4}$ C / / / | / / / / | / / / / | C7 / / / | F7 / / / | / / / / | C / / / |
| / / / / | G7 / / / | / / / / | C / / / | / / / / :‖

Variation 1.

‖: $\frac{4}{4}$ C / / / | / / / / | / / / / | C7 / / / | F / / / | Fm / / / | C / / / |
| A7 / / / | Dm / / / | G7 / / / | C / / / | G7 / / / :‖

Variation 2.

‖: $\frac{4}{4}$ C / / / | F7 / / / | C / / / | C7 / / / | F / / / | F#° / / / |
| C(Pedal G) / / / | A7 / / / | D7 / / / | G7 / / / | C / / / | D♭7 / / / :‖

Key F

‖: $\frac{4}{4}$ F / / / | / / / / | / / / / | F7 / / / | B♭7 / / / | / / / / | F / / / |
| / / / / | C7 / / / | / / / / | F / / / | / / / / :‖

Variation 1.

‖: $\frac{4}{4}$ F / / / | / / / / | / / / / | F7 / / / | B♭ / / / | B♭m / / / | F / / / |
| D7 / / / | Gm / / / | C7 / / / | F / / / | C7 / / / :‖

Variation 2.

‖: $\frac{4}{4}$ F / / / | B♭7 / / / | F / / / | F7 / / / | B♭ / / / | B° / / / |
| F(Pedal C) / / / | D7 / / / | G7 / / / | C7 / / / | F / / / | G♭7 / / / :‖